UND THE WORLD HAVE

OU ARE ABOUT TO MEET

The children in this book are some of the most anonymous humans on the planet. They will probably never travel more than a day's walk from where they live. But in the last few years, they traveled around the world on the historic reunion tour of the band the Police. Their images peered out at audiences of tens of thousands from onstage screens bigger than the houses they live in.

The hope in their eyes is their gift to us—a light to ignite our optimism, perhaps even our action.

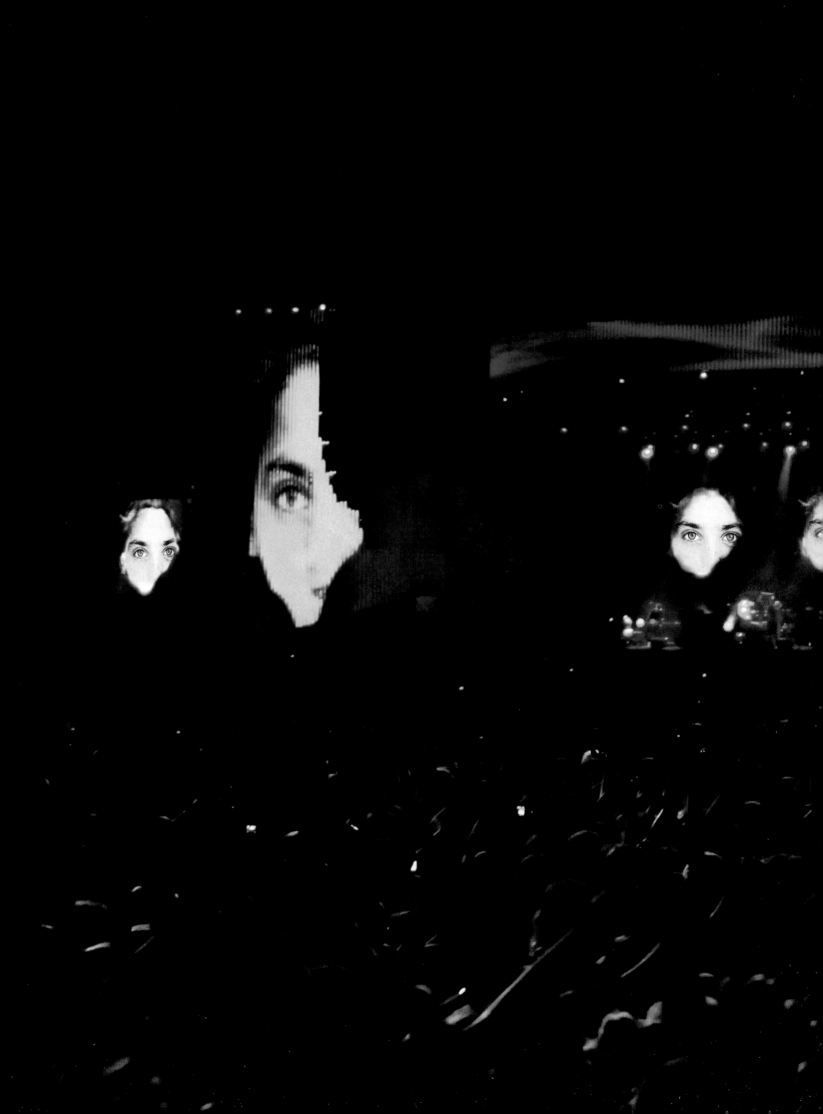

THE POWE
INVISIBL

ROF THE
E SUN

CHRONICLE BOOKS
SAN FRANCISCO

HOPE ISN'T JUST NICE, IT'S A GAME-CHANGER.

I'm writing this at the Hôtel des Mille Collines in Kigali, Rwanda (the "Hotel Rwanda"). Ghosts walk these hallways. Yet 14 years after the genocide, Rwanda is bursting with opportunities and possibilities. Writing about hope from within these tortured walls feels a little eerie but very appropriate. Rwanda's amazing progress is such a poignant example of the power of hope.

Hope is the most important thing that people need to move forward. The slightest ray of hope can ignite the human spirit's ability to overcome: the power of the invisible sun.

Ten years ago I left my work as an entrepreneur to devote myself to philanthropy full-time. Now, along with my wife, Elaine, and my children, Tess and Shane, I travel around the world doing the work of the Sager Family Traveling Foundation and Roadshow.

I met the children in this book during those travels. I photographed them from just weeks after September 11, 2001, until 2009. They live in alleyways, refugee camps, slums, and remote villages from Afghanistan to Rwanda to Nepal. They are refugees, orphans, child soldiers, and just plain kids dealing with war, conflict, natural disaster, abuse, and displacement. I was face-to-face with them because I was there to help, and that's a big part of the connection you see in their eyes.

These kids face daily challenges that bend my spirit and break my heart. Meeting them has made me more thankful and probably a lot more useful.

Even though I have left the business world and spend much of my time helping people, I'm not a do-gooder. I'm a doer who has figured out that hands-on, eyeball-to-eyeball making a difference is a way to live a very full life. Besides, dealing with revolutionaries, political extremists, and blatant opportunists is nothing compared to some of the corporate lawyers I've dealt with.

During my family's years on the road, spending time with famous people and world leaders has provided many wonderful experiences, but the most transcendent moments have come when we least expected them. They've arisen out of the joy and frustration of sharing in ordinary people's everyday lives. In my photography the same is true.

It turns out with both photography and philanthropy that getting as close as possible gets the best results.

I chose to use only images of children for this book because it is through the strength and possibilities you see in their young eyes that the power of the invisible sun becomes so compelling.

Don't feel bad for these kids. They don't want your pity. My motivation in bringing these children together for you to meet is not so you can say, "Oh, look at those poor kids. I want to give them a hug." Hopefully you will take strength from their strength, feel more thankful in your own life, and, in return, go find ways to give people hope, not by just giving money but by giving something of yourself.

Visit these kids and remember the power of the human spirit to overcome. Visit these kids when you need to remember how lucky you are. Visit these kids and ask yourself if you're doing enough to help.

Everyone has to connect their own dots. I hope the experience of this book, in some small way, helps you to connect yours.

—BOBBY SAGER

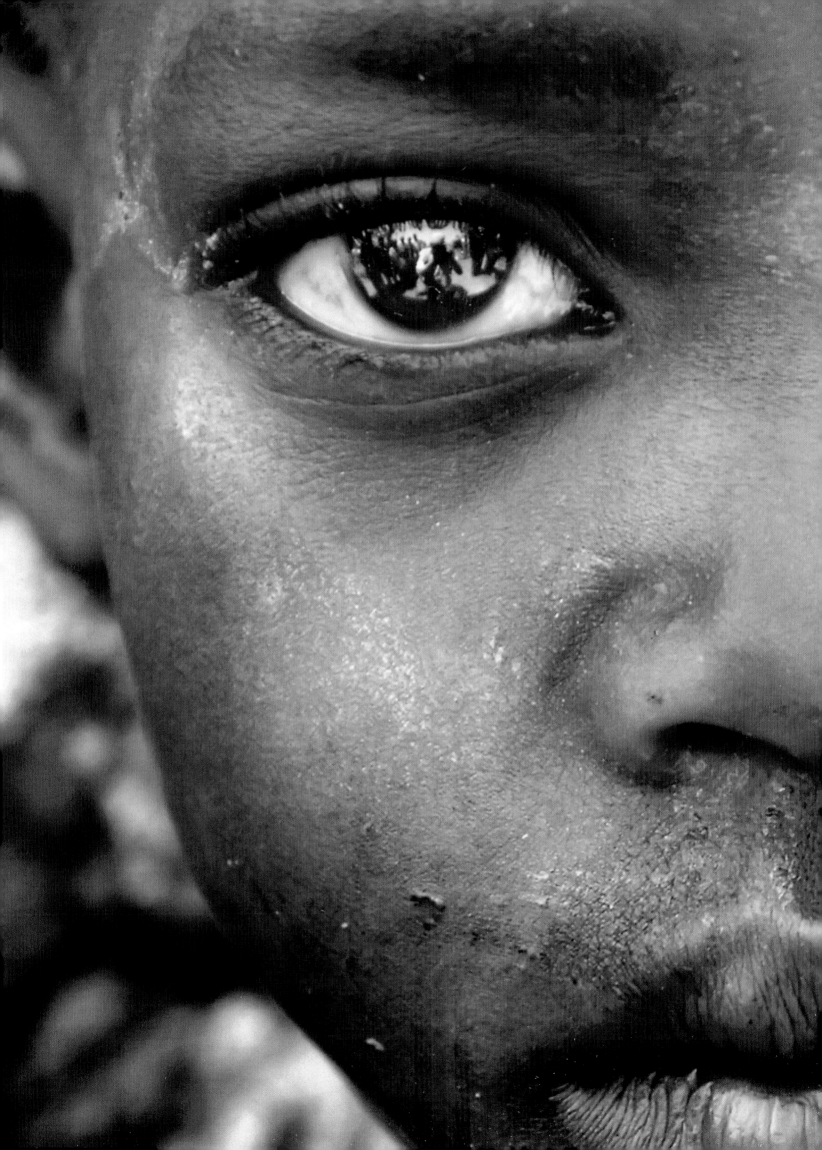

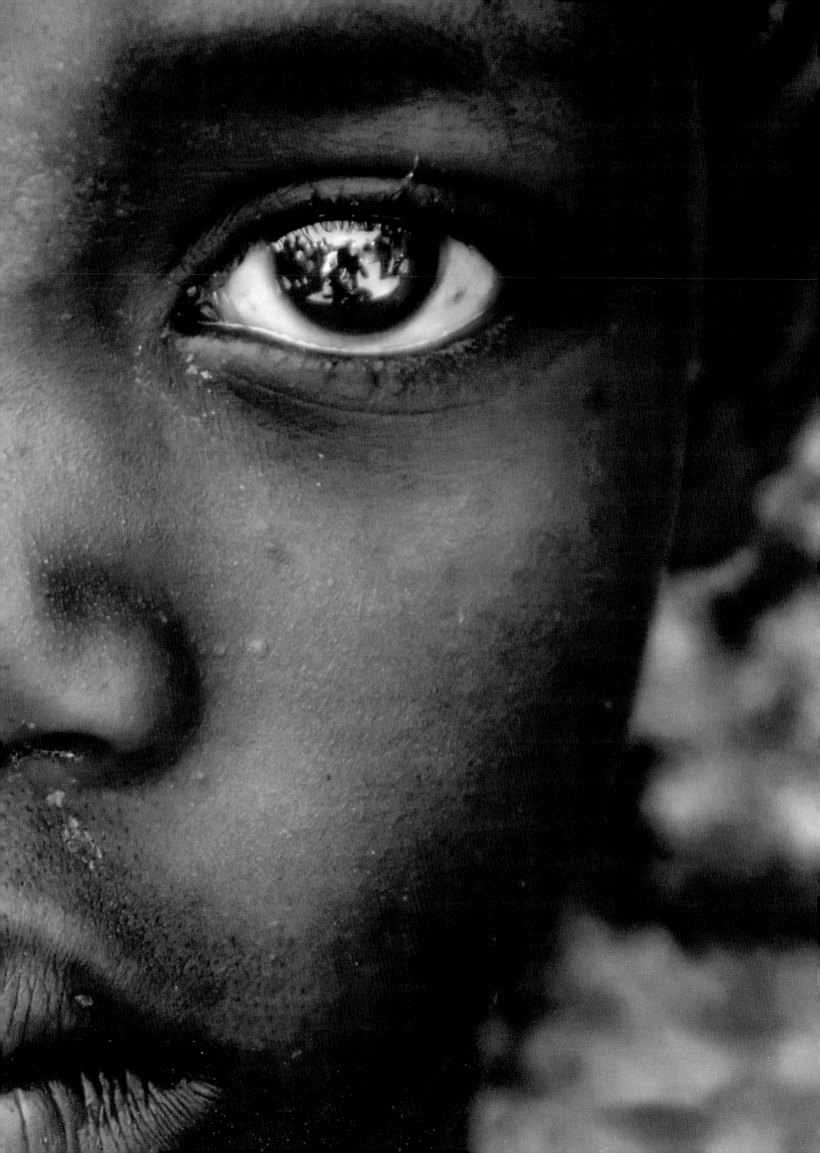

TO SEE THESE CHILDREN LAUGHING IS TO WITNESS THE INVISIBLE SUN MADE VISIBLE.

—STING

"Invisible Sun" was written in the early 1980s. I was living in the west of Ireland at the time, in a Connemara fishing village, on the edge of the Atlantic. The house was surrounded by a seawall that enclosed an acre of land, fine trees of some maturity, a lawn of the greenest turf, and some hardy flowers that could survive the often-harsh coastal weather. Behind the house were the austere mountains of Galway. The setting was beautiful and rugged and inspired me greatly, but it was not an easy time for an Englishman to be living in Ireland.

It was the time of the IRA hunger strikes. Emotions were running high as young men were voluntarily starving themselves to death in protest at what they considered to be the occupation of their country by British forces and their right to be considered "political prisoners." Of course the issues were historical and far more complex than this, but I had enough Irish blood in me to be able to see both sides of this appalling equation. No one side had a monopoly on right or wrong, disgraceful atrocities were committed in the name of "justice" on both sides of the sectarian divide, and there seemed little hope that anything would ever be resolved.

I'd spent some time in the 1970s in Belfast, visiting Andersonstown, an IRA stronghold that was fraught with danger for someone with an English accent. That, coupled with my short hair, put me at risk of being mistaken for a "Squaddie." But my short time there exposed me to the conundrum of the friendliest of communities descending into barbarism and anarchy at a time when lives were filtered through the distorting prism of religious and political extremism, of revenge and blood feuds, and a never-ending cycle of human misery.

I wrote the metaphor of the invisible sun long before there were any peace talks or ideas of power sharing. It was just a dreamer's fantasy that something unseen and beyond our normal awareness was sustaining in us some vague hope for the future, a hope that found a resonance in the human spirit, beyond these dismal streets, beyond the promises and dark threats of our politicians, beyond the dark clouds of our history.

While the song has specific relation to Northern Ireland in the early 1980s, we revisited it for the Police reunion tour of 2007. Though there are of course still tensions, Northern Ireland had entered a hopeful era of peace, and the shooting war is over, one hopes, for good. I was at first a little hesitant to perform the song when we returned to Belfast for a gig on the grounds of Stormont Castle. Like any respectful guest, I was sensitive about not wanting to remind my generous hosts of their recent dark past, but fortunately the song now had some wider terms of reference.

My friend Bobby Sager had been taking photographs of children in war-torn areas such as Afghanistan, Iraq, Rwanda, and the refugee camps of northern Pakistan and Palestine. Their faces are a perfect visual analogue for the song. You can clearly see the anguish and torment in the eyes of those children brought up among violence and injustice, bombs and bullets, but in the next frame (and this is Bobby's genius) the laughter and hope in their eyes when he surprises them with acting the fool, some unexpected zaniness like blowing a raspberry, and engaging them on a simple human level as his right hand clicks away to capture these unforgettable images. This is the invisible sun made visible.

Bobby's photographs accompanied the song on a massive screen behind the stage throughout our tour. Many people said it was the most moving part of the show. Though I was busy facing forward and singing, I couldn't disagree with them—the effect was palpable. The song had been given a new lease on life; a wider, universal context; and, I hope, a prophetic vision of a better future for all the world's children.

    There has to be an invisible sun
    That gives its heat to everyone.

—STING

MARACANÃ STADIUM, RIO DE JANEIRO, BRAZIL, 2008

PREVIOUS << JALALABAD, AFGHANISTAN, 2001
NEXT >> RIVER PLATE STADIUM, BUENOS AIRES, ARGENTINA, 2007

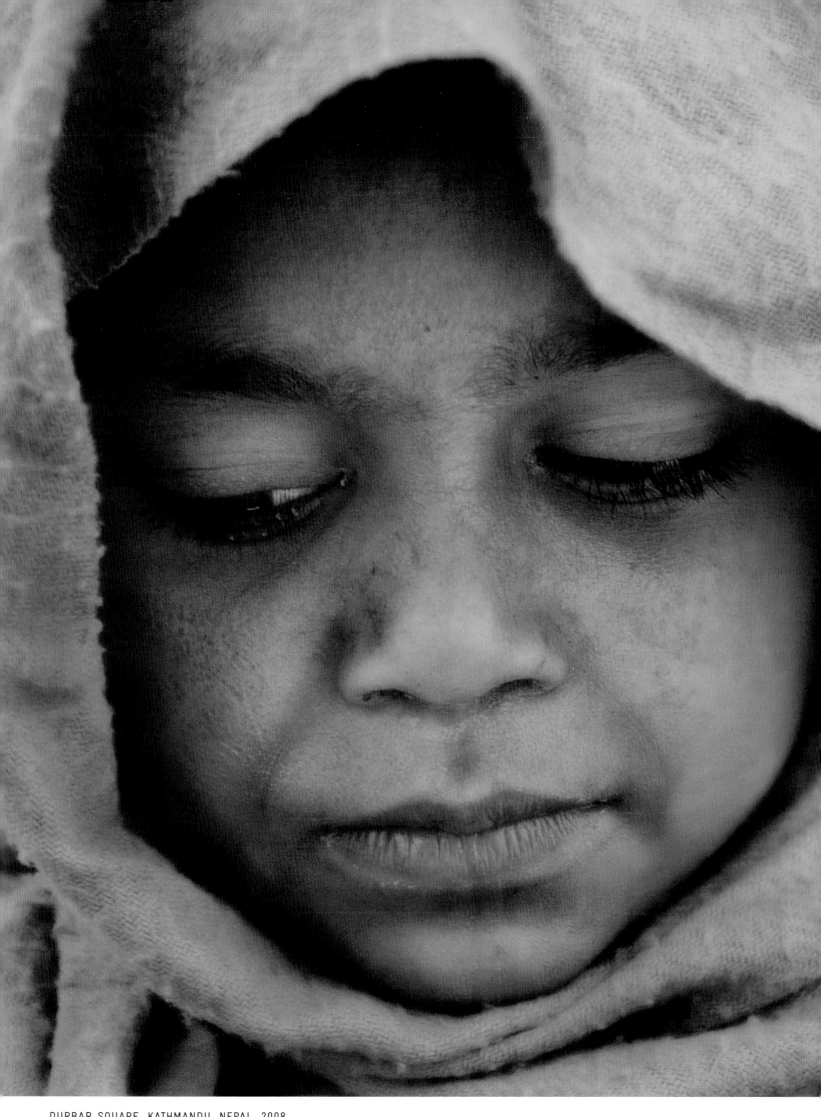

DURBAR SQUARE, KATHMANDU, NEPAL, 2008

NEAR EID-GAH MOSQUE, KABUL, AFGHANISTAN, 2002 / I came across these kids in a bombed-out neighborhood in Kabul. There was so much sadness and distance in their eyes. Then I made a fart sound by doing a raspberry with my mouth. This photograph shows the boys' reaction to the camera. The next photograph is their reaction to me. It's the human connection that is so special. The photograph is just a by-product.

KABUL, AFGHANISTAN, 2002 / The kids on the preceding pages live
just to the left of these buildings.

PREVIOUS << KACHA GARI REFUGEE CAMP, NORTH-WEST
FRONTIER PROVINCE (NWFP), PAKISTAN, 2001 / About a month
after September 11.

KACHA GARI REFUGEE CAMP, NWFP, PAKISTAN / This school was one of
only two high schools for girls in all the Afghan refugee camps in the
NWFP. No roof, no lights, no heat, no furniture—just desire.

This letter, and others throughout the book, are parts of handwritten notes that I sent to family and friends from the road while I was taking these pictures. I hope they give you a little more context with which to think about the photographs.

KABUL Afghanistan / Jan 7, 2004

It's tough to be an American on the Road nowadays, I've been on the ground in a dozen or so countries in the last 6 months real low to the ground and at the highest levels—The feedback on U.S. policy has been consistently suspicious, negative and utterly unconvinced of our official purpose and justification. Comments are not limited to IRAQ—They include Kyoto Agreements, World Court, United Nations, Ballistic treaties and lots more.

Assumptions are where the rubber meets the road. Do the official assumptions underlying our actions stand-up to reasonable scrutiny or not? Through history so much conflict and missed opportunity have resulted from bad assumptions, poor listening and unintended consequences.

The United States has the potential to do earthshakingly great things but from out here it feels like we are about to blow it in a blur of self-absorbed, holier than thou simplistic bullshit (I have to pay my kids $.25 each time I swear but I can't think of a better word than bullshit so I'll just have to pay the fine.)

Is the bottom line power or something much more benign, long term and constructive like influence? I'm concerned that we are fast losing our ability to influence by not listening and by clumsily exerting our power.

With so much of our attention focused on IRAQ it seems like we aren't thinking nearly enough about critical issues like the economy, Healthcare education or the environment. Are we listening to the loudest noise and not paying attention to the issues most critical to our long term common welfare? I hope the noise dies down so that we can start to listen to our hearts. They're hard to hear through all the static.

KHYBER PASS, FEDERALLY ADMINISTERED TRIBAL AREA, PAKISTAN–AFGHANISTAN BORDER, 2001

NEXT >> KABUL, AFGHANISTAN, 2001

KABUL, AFGHANISTAN, NOVEMBER 2002

NEXT >> The view from the back of this girl's house.

CHILD SOLDIER REHABILITATION CAMP, RUHENGERI, RWANDA, 2005 / Moises was a soldier in the Congo. He killed three people when he was seven years old.

NEXT >> RUHENGERI, RWANDA, 2005 / This soccer ball is Moises's prized possession.

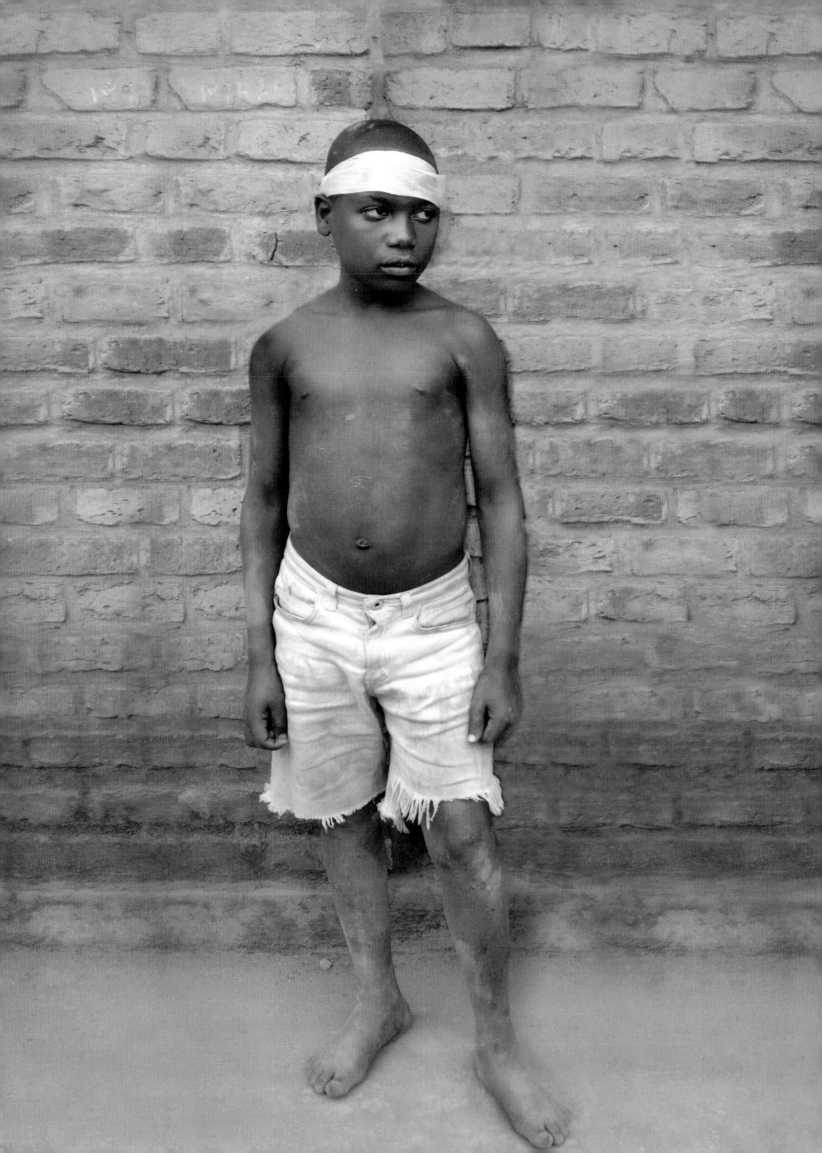

LAKE MUGHEZI, RWANDA, 2008 / Child soldier recently
returned from the Congo.

Manshera PAKISTAN / Jan 6, 2006

ON Oct 8th a 7.6 magnitude earthquake struck the Northern areas of pakistan and KASHMIR. OVER 80,000 people were killed (including 17,000 children) 100,000 people were injured 8000 Schools destroyed and over 3 million people were left homeless. The Scale of the disaster is Staggering.

Elaine, Tess shane and I came to PAKISTAN to bring blankets to the victims - the devastation is Shocking and we can feel the Severe winter all around US.

people are understandably dazed but even in the midst of the mind numbing destruction there is Virtually No begging - people are appreciative and proud - Supporting each other with a Strong but quiet dignity.

The pakistani Army has really stood up to be counted in this crisis, specifically an incredibly commited Brigadier Namal Khslid who has agreed to utilize his logistical Assets (helicopters, trucks, communication equipment, etc) to help us get the blankets to the progressively less accessible high mountain areas - I have seen first hand that this is a guy that knows how to get stuff done -

The inhabitants of this area are a fiercely proud people with intense and devout ideas about honor, family and friendship. Before oct 8th 3 million people that had homes now live in tents amidst the penetrating cold. TAlk about a fundamental change of circumstance - Think a blanket especially for children or elderly trying to survive the winter could be high impact?

A Blanket is an act of compassion a great blanket is a sign of respect IN a Seperate letter we will provide details on how you could TAp into the delivery sytem we are building and supply blankets as well

KIBERA, NAIROBI, KENYA, 2006

PREVIOUS << ZIMBABWE, 2004
NEXT >> GOSPEL CHURCH OF POWER, KHAYELITSHA, SOUTH
AFRICA, 2006

CENTRAL MARKET, KABUL, AFGHANISTAN, 2003

CENTRAL MARKET, KIGALI, RWANDA, 2003

TIBETAN CHILDREN'S VILLAGE, DHARAMSALA, INDIA,
FEBRUARY 2004

NEXT >> LO MANTHANG, KINGDOM OF MUSTANG / Seven days'
walk from the end of the closest road. The mountains in the back-
ground are in Tibet.

TIBETAN REFUGEE CAMP #4, NEAR SERA JEY MONASTERY,
BYLAKUPPE, SOUTH INDIA, 2005

NEXT >> LO MANTHANG, KINGDOM OF MUSTANG, 2006

Kathmandu Nepal / April 21, 03

Hello from deep in The Third world

I'm sitting in The faded ballroom of a wondrously broken down 100 year old Hotel, We've stayed here on and off for a dozen years It's one of our many homes away from home, I'm writing This at The U shaped table set up for tomorrows scheduled restart of peace talks between The Government and the Maoist Rebels, - Thousands of Nepalese have died and The Normal life of the Country has been brought to its knees

Nepal is both tragic and magical ~~~~~~ nestled against the Himalaya The mongols of the North blend with the Aryans from The South and what man is seems at once ancient and fluid- Physical distinctions fade into the essential being - How much learning floats by us everyday when we fail to recognize genius because of preconceived notions That people with less education or less money or less "accomplishment" have less insight?

Yesterday I sat in a vast outdoor Hindu temple, Sadhu Holymen and half-crazed monkeys Still around me, The burning embers from a human cremation hung in the dark air like fireflies - The smoke and smell of burning flesh enveloped me, In The end we are the same puff of smoke The same essential being yet we keep killing each other over differences in The way we think or practice religion or conduct politics,

I know its way too utopian to think That we will all ever just hug and love each other - but proactively dealing with hate Could be as important to the future of the planet as clean water. This isn't touchy feely stuff - we need to find much better ways to tactically deal with prejudice - Understanding and tolerance are the DNA of lasting peace,

INTERNALLY DISPLACED PERSONS CAMP, NWFP, PAKISTAN, 2005 /
After the earthquake. This boy lives in the tented camp on the following pages. He's so proud of his toy.

NEXT >> PAKISTAN, 2005 / Some of the 3 million who lost their homes.

PREVIOUS << INTERNALLY DISPLACED PERSONS CAMP, NWFP, PAKISTAN, 2005 / The girl on the previous pages lives in this camp; somehow she's still smiling.

PAKISTAN, AFTER THE EARTHQUAKE, 2005 / The tidy front yards are such a heartbreaking attempt at normalcy and dignity.

KABUL, AFGHANISTAN, 2002 / This girl lives next to the mosque on the following pages. Imagine still having such optimism in your eyes.

NEXT >> KABUL, AFGHANISTAN, 2002

KABUL, AFGHANISTAN, 2004

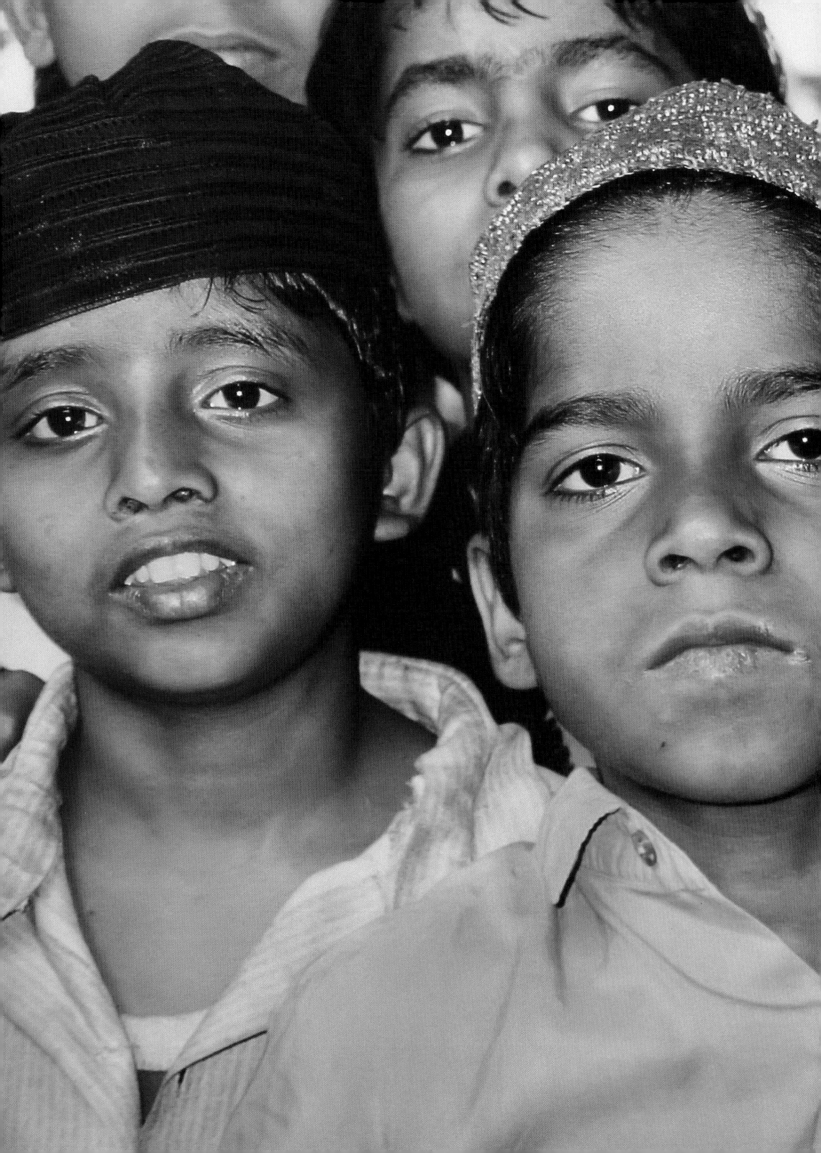

MUSLIM SCHOOL, WELIGAMA, SRI LANKA, 2001

NEXT >> WELIGAMA, SRI LANKA, 2001 / These fishing spots are passed down from father to son.

GALLE, SRI LANKA, 2001 / Galle was later devastated by the 2004 tsunami

Peshawer Pakistan / Oct, 23, 2001

I've just returned to Peshawer from the Afghan border. I know that some (or all) of you think I am insane for being here right now. All I can say is that you are probably right — But being here now and trying to help has given people I have met some hope, confidence and comfort at a time when they really need it.

I wasn't thinking I could change the situation in some grand way — I didn't know what I may be able to do to help but I was pretty sure I needed to come to have a chance of figuring anything out. The combination of being the personal guest of the Governor of the N.W. Frontier province, my personal persuasive powers and the fact that nobody else is whacked out enough to be here now have combined to make me the first non-journalist to be given permission to travel through the Khyber Pass and the Tribal Areas since the bombing started — It has been a shattering sometimes scary but very rich experience.

I saw a little girl writhing on a cement floor with a broken back another girl started screaming uncontrolably and running in circles as a plane flew overhead. A bomb had fallen a few miles away a few days before. A 10 yr. old girl stood up in one of the refugee schools I visited and through tears asked me how the USA could destroy her country because of only one man — Her eyes probed mine as I fumbled through an attempt at an answer.

I Realize that war is Hell and that innocent people will inevitably be affected — but being in the middle of the misery made me realize just how far ranging the victims of Sept 11th really are. Post Sept 11 is certainly about our safety but it is also very much about our soul. — How do we encounter and engage evil without losing a little of our own humanity?

NEXT >> NORTHERN AFGHANISTAN, 2004 / On the road to Mazār-e Sharif.

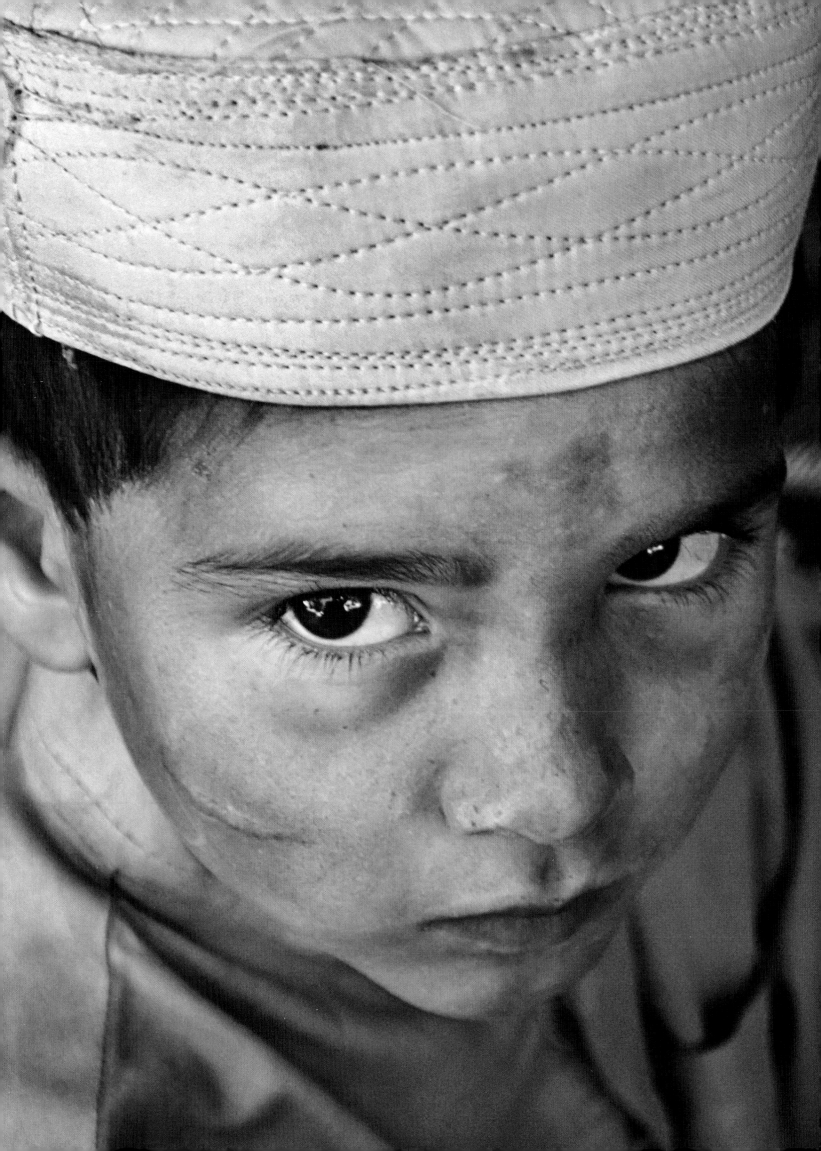

KABUL, AFGHANISTAN, 2002 / Taliban Ministry of Information.

AFGHAN REFUGEE CAMP, OCTOBER 2001 / Their village had been
bombed a few weeks before.

NEXT >> UNITED NATIONS HIGH COMMISSIONER FOR REFUGEES
(UNHCR) CAMP, 2001 / This camp was home to 50,000 Afghans.

RWANDA, 2008

NEXT >> NEAR LAKE MUGHEZI, RWANDA, 2008

PREVIOUS << NEAR MURAMBI, RWANDA, 2005   CHURCH, NTARAMA, RWANDA, 2005 / In 1994 an estimated 2,500
people were murdered here during the genocide.

RUHENGERI, RWANDA, 2005

A NOTE TO 15,000 FELLOW LEADERS:

In the ongoing effort of the YPO Presidents' Action Network to opportunistically connect members from different sides of conflicts around the world, we came up with the idea of hosting the first-ever joint meeting between the Israel and Palestine Chapter at Sting's concert in Tel Aviv. Almost the entire Palestinian and Israeli membership attended.

Since our night in Tel Aviv, a whole new round of violence has spiraled to the edge of darkness, which makes it easy to find reasons not to engage and to believe that there is no one on the other side to talk to. Bad things will continue to happen. It's what we do about it that makes the difference. We simply can't sit around waiting for political leaders to sort things out.

Vigorously pursuing peace could yield the ultimate in kick-ass return on investment for our families, businesses, and communities. As entrepreneurs, we have the ability to help. With our incredible Rolodexes, we have the responsibility to help.

Anyway, here is what happened . . .

As I arrived at the stadium, my thoughts drifted to what the Palestinians and Israelis must have been thinking about as they drove through the traffic of Tel Aviv to this historic event. The Palestinians were braving the indignities and sheer inconvenience of Israeli roadblocks to drive from Ramallah to Tel Aviv. Some may have even faced the scorn of their community for "normalizing the occupation" by even talking to Israelis. In attendance was an Israeli member whose family had been murdered by a suicide bomber. Members from both sides were nevertheless willing to engage, just because it may help to make things better—no guarantees. Isn't that what leadership is about?

There is someone on the "other side" to talk to. I have met them from both sides, and their voices are heard by many others, including their leaders.

As the Israelis and the Palestinians mingled over hors d'oeuvres and drinks before the concert, I surveyed the room and thought to myself how similar they actually are. Same strong ideas about family and education. Very passionate. Great negotiators. Strong-willed. So much that is the same, with so much focus on the differences. A kind of cousins. It always seems like some of the biggest fights are fights within families.

So often, attempted exchanges of ideas deteriorate to the point where whoever stops to breathe first is the one that loses the argument.

We spent the next three hours LISTENING to each other, trying to understand more, and maybe with that understanding gain some real insight, and with that insight, plus the power of our network, make a difference—maybe just with our family and friends, maybe through local and national leaders.

Now it was time to party. Thanks to Sting we were escorted to a special area directly in front of the stage restricted for riot control. The separate groups from Palestine and Israel soon melted into one, feeling the beat.

No filters. So many of the problems in the region result from the distorting filters of the media and the rhetoric of religious and political leaders. We may disagree, but we at least listen, look each other in the eye, and know each other as human beings, not stereotypes.

Like almost any deal, peace in the Middle East won't happen without the sides agreeing to some leap of faith; and just as in business, no one takes a leap of faith without some level of confidence in who they are dealing with.

There are of course extremists on both sides. That's why it is so important in the midst of the spiraling chaos of the last month not to react in ways that energize the extremists' position and drown out the many voices of reason. It's about hearts and minds. Why don't our strategies focus on this? How about economic opportunity; what are we doing as entrepreneurs to help?

Are we willing to make the same kind of passionate commitment to pursuing peace that extremists devote to their causes? We need smarter ways, worldwide, to fight extremism. So far the strategy and execution are weak.

The Germans killed 20 million Russians in World War II, and they are now each other's biggest trading partners. Common opportunity in a dynamic regional economy could become an essential part of a lasting peace. So much comes down to feeding one another's reasonable self-interest around business, family, and opportunity. Who cares if reconciliation is for selfish reasons? Enlightened self-interest is sustainable. We are business leaders. We may not be able to make peace in the Middle East, but we can help to create the conditions where peace is more likely and more sustainable.

In the midst of so much disappointment and frustration, it is hard to find positive ways forward. But throwing up our hands is just not acceptable. Concrete baby steps matter, even if it is just to keep us all sane. I hope you find your own baby steps. When we add them all together—who knows? At a minimum we can look our kids in the eye and tell them we really tried.

Being "right" but rigid is no way forward.

On a hot night in Tel Aviv, a remarkable bunch of young leaders who care more about the future of their kids than they do about religious dogma, and who care more about people than they do about politics, came together, looked each other in the eye, and had a little fun.

Whoever says "it's only rock 'n' roll" has never danced with the Israelis and the Palestinians.

—BOBBY SAGER

(The Young Presidents' Organization (YPO) is a worldwide network of thousands of mostly 30- to 50-year-old presidents of multimillion-dollar businesses. If you were to add together the annual sales of their businesses and convert it to GDP dollars, YPO would be the third-largest economy in the world.)

QALANDIA, WEST BANK, 2005 / I love her nails. She's just trying to be a little girl.

NEXT >> QALANDIA, WEST BANK, 2009 / This checkpoint between Jerusalem and Ramallah is near the home of the girl on page 107.

FASAYIL VILLAGE, JORDAN VALLEY, WEST BANK, MARCH 2009

NEXT >> JORDAN VALLEY NEAR JERICHO, WEST BANK, 2008

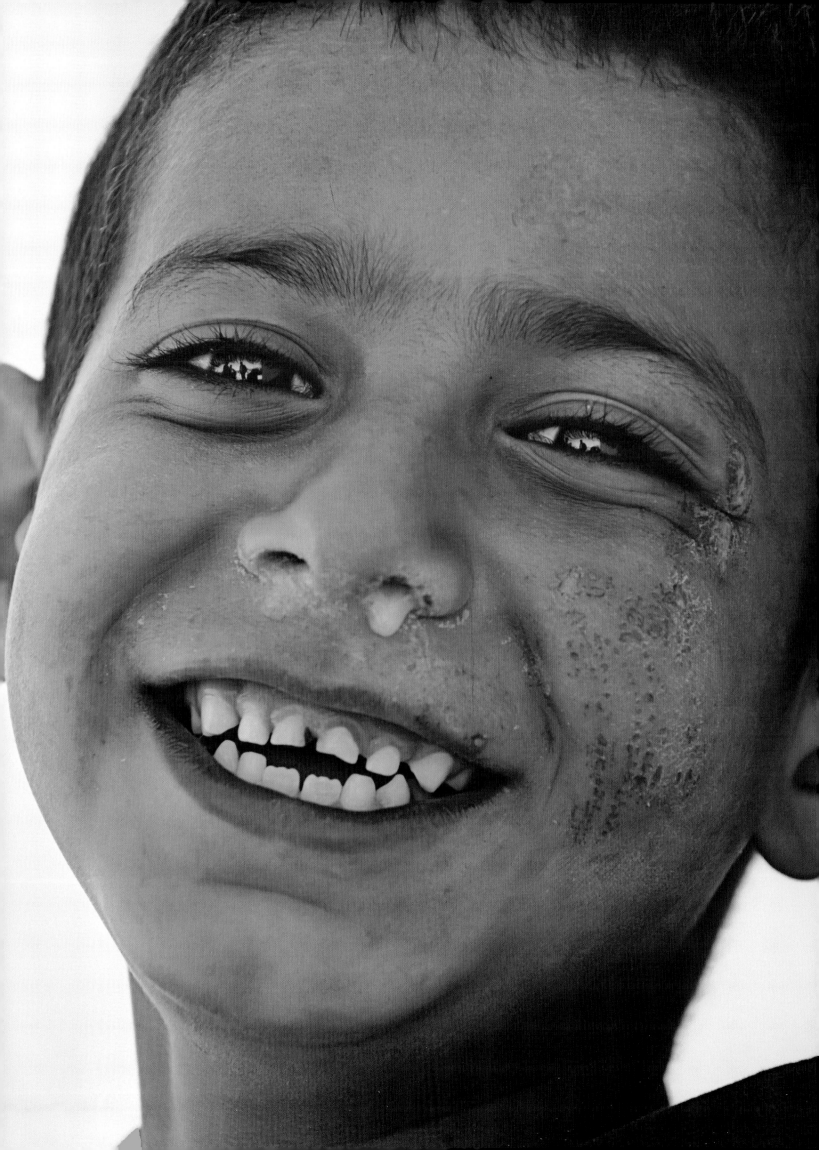

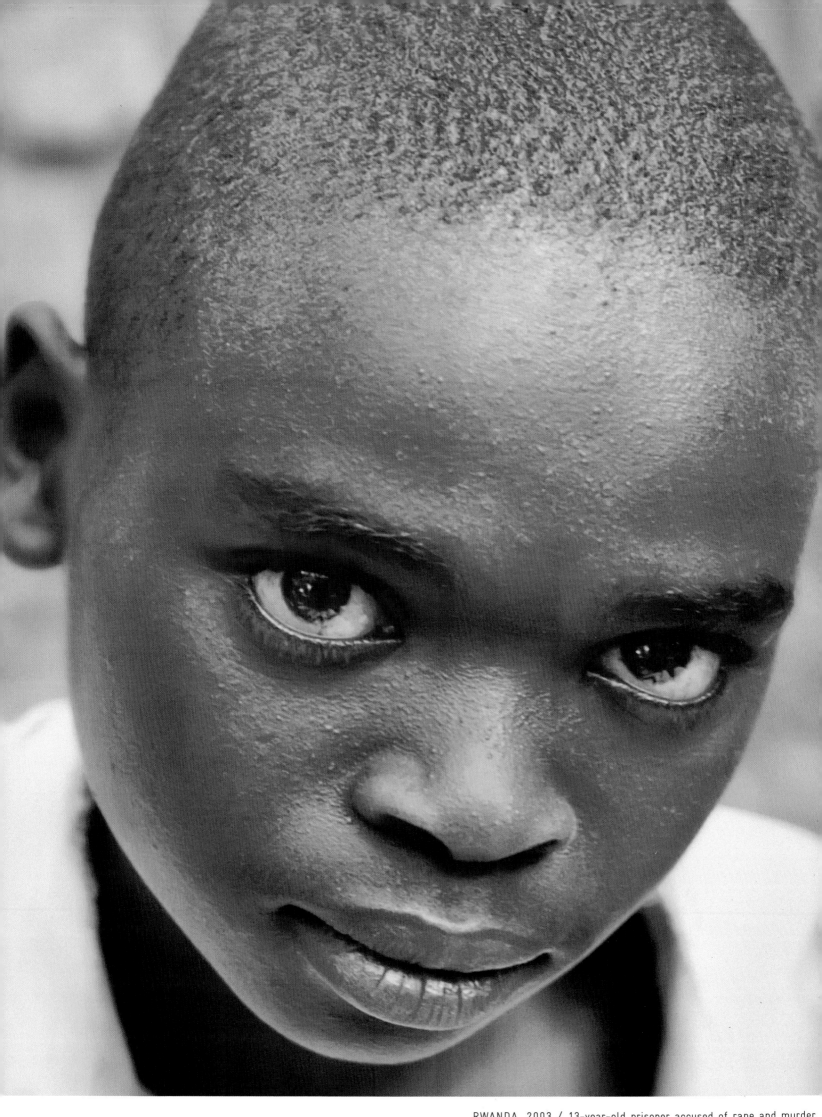

RWANDA, 2003 / 13-year-old prisoner accused of rape and murder.

RWANDA, 2007 / 13-year-old student.

RWANDA, 2004 / Orphanage.

CENTRAL PRISON, KIGALI, RWANDA, 2007 / This little girl lives with her
mother in jail. The inner door to the jail's courtyard is about to close for the night.

BALAKOT, NWFP, PAKISTAN, DECEMBER 2005 / Just two months after the earthquake of October 2005. Eighty percent of homes were destroyed in this girl's town. But even in the midst of the mind-numbing devastation, there is still a strength of spirit and a smile in her eyes.

NEXT >> NORTHERN KABUL, AFGHANISTAN, 2001 / Her face was burned by an Allied or American bomb.

What did you and I get pissed off about today? It probably doesn't compare to her daily challenges.

It's hard to be happy unless you're thankful, and it's difficult to be thankful without some context to appreciate what you have. The kids in this book provide context on steroids.

I hope that meeting the kids in this book has given you more perspective on the challenges you face in your own life and, as a result, helps you to be more thankful and more ready to find ways to make a difference in the lives of others. Maybe you will, maybe you won't, but maybe you will.

FROM "I CAN'T MAKE A DIFFERENCE"
TO "YOUR CONCRETE BABY STEPS MATTER"

NO MORE OUTSOURCING.

It used to be that we could outsource fixing the world to governments and large organizations. Today it's clear that individuals must actively engage in making a difference. It's no longer just helpful and nice, it's critical. If your response is, "yeah, but the world's problems are just too big and there's nothing I can do," then I would encourage you to think about the power of "concrete baby steps."

A concrete baby step is not a token effort; it's a tangible, usually hands-on response to a problem. Concrete baby steps are relatively easy to see individually, but it's hard to fathom their cumulative power. When we each take a concrete baby step, and we add up mine and yours and everyone else's, they can become the building blocks of transformational change. In fact, collectively, concrete baby steps may be the best solution we have to address the world's biggest problems.

I once heard a fascinating speaker ask, "How many seeds are there in an apple?" As the audience fumbled through some answers, he observed: "While you can find out how many seeds are in an apple quite easily by simply cutting it open and counting them, you can never know how many apples, or even trees, could one day sprout from just one of those seeds."

A new idea is a seed. Looking someone you are trying to help in the eye is a seed. Letting people know they have value as a human being is a seed. Taking a concrete baby step is a seed. If you think that the world's problems are too big and there's nothing you can do to make a difference, start by planting a seed. Who knows how many orchards it may one day yield.

Giving someone hope is the ultimate seed. A little bit of hope changes everything: all the odds, all the upside. Lots more people win. Just do the math.

FROM SELFLESSNESS
TO SELFISHNESS

HANDS-ON HELPING IS SUCH A WONDERFUL GIFT TO GIVE YOURSELF.

People often tell me how impressed they are that, after my
business success, I am now so committed to giving back to
society. Invariably someone tells me what a wonderful, selfless
person I am.

The truth is, I sleep in tents, shit in holes, and expose
myself to all kinds of risks and frustrations because I'm
selfish.

By being on the ground, face-to-face with the people we are
trying to help, my family and I get to live amazing life moments,
learning, feeling, and accomplishing. That's what I mean by
being selfish.

The idea that people give to charity because they are sup-
posed to isn't sustainable, and people who need help deserve
real long-term commitment. Finding ways to serve your self-
interest fuels that commitment.

Far from the tradition of writing a check and going to the
annual dinner, being hands-on, looking people in their eyes,
feeling their humanity, and letting them feel yours isn't just
helping, it's a way to live life to the fullest. And that's the
best return on investment I've ever gotten by a long shot.

I'm selfish, and I'm not ashamed to say it, because the
more selfish I am, the more impact I make on people who need
my help.

Whether it is on the other side of the world or just
around the corner, so much learning, living, and feeling flows
out of the intense human connection that comes from being able
to touch the people you are trying to help. As a result of
serving my self-interest, I end up giving much more. Talk about
win-win. Just do the math.

FROM CHARITY
TO PHILANTHROPY

HANDS-UP NOT HAND-OUTS

For me, philanthropic return on investment is about making the
biggest impact possible on fellow human beings, regardless of
country, race, or religion. It often entails going to the most
screwed-up places, because that's where the gap between current
reality and what most people would consider minimally acceptable
is enormous, so there is lots of upside; and where money goes
very far, so there is lots of potential impact. My family and I
live close to the ground so that we truly understand what's
going on and so that I can use my entrepreneurial ability,
instincts, and tenacity to get really tough stuff done. Money
certainly matters, but when we make ourselves the currency, it
matters even more.

But this isn't warm and fuzzy helping. My family and I are
not about simply hugging and helping poor people around the
world. We demand accountability and strategic ways of thinking
and acting. Screw giving an "A" for effort. Helping others is
too important to not be very demanding of the result. There's a
way to give that sustains and a way that creates dependency.

Forget the mindset that the rich do business and the poor
get charity. Charity doesn't make people feel good about themselves and can cripple generations. But the biggest problem is
that it's not sustainable.

You've probably heard the old adage: If you give a hungry
man a fish, he will eat for a day. If you give him a fishing
pole and teach him to fish, he will eat for a lifetime. Giving
the fish is charity. Giving the fishing pole is the beginning of
helping people to help themselves.

But while it's clear that it's better to give a hungry man a
fishing pole than a fish, unless you also teach him how to sell
the fish, all he is ever going to be able to do is eat fish!

The poor have a tremendous amount of creativity and are
well equipped for business, but they need help getting started.
Help can be something as specific as a microenterprise program
to something as broad as a decent education. But it needs to be
systemic. No one-shot, feel-good stuff.

It's the difference between simply giving and really helping.
It's about investing in people. Just do the math.

AFTER THE EARTHQUAKE, NWFP, PAKISTAN, JANUARY 2005 / Tess and Shane, Christmas vacation.

MY HERO IS NOT NECESSARILY THE PRESIDENT OF A COUNTRY OR A PRIME MINISTER OR A CABINET MINISTER. IT IS SOMEBODY WHO HAS DECLARED WAR ON POVERTY, ON DISEASE, ON ILLITERACY, AND WHO IS PREPARED TO GIVE HUMAN BEINGS HOPE THAT THERE IS A FUTURE FOR HIM OR HER. THOSE ARE MY HEROES.

—NELSON MANDELA, at his home in Johannesburg in 2003, answering Tess's question about who his heroes are

RWANDA, 2008 / All these prisoners participated in the genocide.
The guy on the left killed 30 people.

We have spent a few days acclimatizing in and around Katmandu, waiting for helicopter weather, as well as for the arrival of my friend Bobby Sager, an old Nepal hand, flamboyant eccentric, inexhaustible world traveler, and practical philanthropist. It was Bobby who suggested Nepal as a destination, and specifically Lo Manthang . . .

The manicured lawn in front of the hotel is a welcome oasis inside the turmoil of the city. (My friend) Simon (Astaire), (my son,) Jake, and I are sipping a genteel afternoon tea after a tiring day, when the tranquil scene is broken by a loud banging and a maniacal hollering from the back of a pickup truck that has roared through the open gates in a cloud of dust. There on the back is what can be described only as a psychedelic vision, a Martian in wrap-around shades and a flowing tie-dyed monk's robe of orange and yellow, with a blue, sparkling bandana tied pirate-fashion around his head, arms outstretched like some messiah entering a conquered city. Bobby Sager, my old friend, has made his entrance, and even the crows are transfixed by this vision . . .

"What the fuck is that?" says Simon, who has never met Bobby before.

"That is Bobby Sager," I tell him. "And nothing I could have said about him would have prepared you for the experience, so welcome to Planet Bobby . . ."

I met this cyclone of a man four years ago in Brazil. He wanted me to help him get into the interior of the rain forest, where the tourists don't go, so I gave him a few of my contacts and we kept in touch.

Bobby began his working life scalping tickets to Boston Celtics games and ended up buying the hallowed parquet floor of the Boston Garden, before it was torn down. He had made a fortune or three before the age of 40, and now he spends his time roaming the planet looking for projects to support that will, in his words, "make a difference." He's funding the reconstruction of a monastery in Bhutan, helping the Dalai Lama's religious scholars learn science, setting up teacher training programs for Afghan refugees, assisting the people of Rwanda in rebuilding their justice system after the appalling massacres that have all but destroyed their country, and running microenterprise programs in South Africa, Nepal, and Rwanda . . .

Our practical philanthropist spends the rest of the day photographing children in the village and teaching Jake some of his secrets. He has a breathtaking series of what he calls "children in conflict" portraits, of children in Afghanistan, in refugee camps in Pakistan and Rwanda, of Tibetan refugees in camps in India, and of Palestinian refugees in Lebanon.

I watch him work. Sitting just outside a group of youngsters, he begins an animated conversation with a mischievous glove puppet, a bright yellow duck. He whispers to it to be quiet and well behaved; the duck nods in obedience and then proceeds to attack Bobby, who only barely manages to control his tiny adversary. The children begin to stare at the strange sight of this big man and his recalcitrant duck, laughing uproariously when the duck gets the better of him. They move closer, and the duck starts to tease the children. Some of them run away giggling; others get closer.

"Never start taking pictures immediately," he tells Jake. "You've got to engage them, make them laugh, get close." Without looking through the lens he casually takes some shots of the children laughing. "The closer you get, the better the pictures, but don't ever lose eye contact."

I watch as my son engages with the children, making them laugh, coaxing the shy ones to break out of their shells, until Bobby starts chasing the entire gaggle of children around the town square like an overgrown kid, whooping and roaring as the children scatter hilariously and hide behind their mothers' long skirts.

A young man attempts to give Bobby a can of some soft drink, saying something in Nepalese.

"Pema, what the hell's the kid saying? Why's he trying to give me this can?"

Pema talks to the boy, who is about 12. "He says you saved his grandmother's life last year, Mr. Bobby. She needed an operation in Katmandu, and you put her in the helicopter. He says the family wants to thank you, and this is all they have to give you."

The big brash guy from Boston is suddenly quiet and clearly touched by the gesture. My two abiding memories of this extraordinary and complex man will be of him chasing the village kids like the town fool one minute, and the next reduced almost to tears by this simple gift.

—STING

Very often a book's "Special Thanks" becomes a laundry list of people important to the author. My thanks is singularly dedicated to my wife, Elaine. Without Elaine's willingness to live so much of our life on the road in very difficult circumstances and to encourage my efforts when I travel alone, I would not have been in a position to meet so many of the kids in this book.

"Special Thanks" doesn't even seem like nearly enough appreciation for the opportunity to live so much, to feel so much, and to make such a difference.

NOT EVERYTHING THAT CAN BE COUNTED COUNTS, AND NOT EVERYTHING THAT COUNTS CAN BE COUNTED.

—ALBERT EINSTEIN

BE SELFISH, GO HELP SOMEONE.

ADDITIONAL CAPTIONS:

COVER / EID-GAH MOSQUE, KABUL, AFGHANISTAN, 2002

PAGE 6 / KHYBER PASS, FEDERALLY ADMINISTERED TRIBAL
AREA, AFGHANISTAN-PAKISTAN BORDER, 2000

PAGE 8 / KABUL, AFGHANISTAN, OCTOBER 2002

PAGES 10–11 / BUTARE, RWANDA, 2005

PAGE 12 / NEAR BAGRAM AIR BASE, AFGHANISTAN, 2004

PAGES 124–125 / AFGHAN REFUGEE PROCESSING CENTER,
PAKISTAN, OCTOBER 2001

PAGE 134 / NEPAL, 2003

PAGE 138 / BALAKOT, NWFP, PAKISTAN, 2005

PAGE 140 / PESHAWAR, PAKISTAN, 2001

PAGE 142 / BHAKTAPUR, NEPAL, 2004

ENDPAPERS / BELGRADE, SERBIA, 2008

BACK COVER / AFGHAN REFUGEE PROCESSING CENTER,
PAKISTAN, OCTOBER 2001

ALL OF THE AUTHOR'S PROCEEDS FROM THIS BOOK ARE GOING
TO SUPPORT PHILANTHROPIC INITIATIVES AROUND THE WORLD.
PLEASE VISIT WWW.POWEROFTHEINVISIBLESUN.ORG FOR MORE
INFORMATION ABOUT THESE PROGRAMS.

Copyright © 2009 by The Sager Family Traveling Foundation and Road Show, Inc.

"Invisible Sun" lyrics on page 15 reprinted with permission. Words and Lyrics by
Sting. Copyright © 1981 Gordon Sumner, Administered by EMI Music Publishing, Ltd.

Essay on page 137 is an excerpt from "Walking on the Moon," by Sting from Men's
Journal, November 2003. Copyright © Men's Journal LLC 2003. All Rights Reserved.
Reprinted by Permission.

ISBN 978-0-8118-7912-5
Library of Congress Cataloging-in-Publication Data available under
ISBN 978-0-8118-7297-3.

Manufactured in China.
Design by Tumbleweed Design, NY
Letters from the Road illustrated by Bobby Sager.
This book has been set in DIN, Trixie, and GRAVUR.

Photo on page 136 by Tess Sager.

10 9 8 7 6 5 4 3 2 1

Chronicle Books LLC
680 Second Street
San Francisco, California 94107
www.chroniclebooks.com/custom

www.teamsager.org